Wild and Woolly Mammoths

for Flo Stone

Wild and Woolly Mammoths

written and illustrated by

ALIKI

A Harper Trophy Book

Thomas Y. Crowell Company • New York

LET'S-READ-AND-FIND-OUT BOOKS

Let's-Read-and-Find-Out Books are edited by Dr. Roma Gans, Professor Emeritus of Childhood Education, Teachers College, Columbia University, and Dr. Franklyn M. Branley, Astronomer Emeritus and former Chairman of the American Museum–Hayden Planetarium. Text and illustrations for each of the more than 100 books in the series are checked for accuracy by an expert in the relevant field. Other titles available in paperback are listed below. Look for them at your local bookstore or library.

A Baby Starts to Grow	*How Many Teeth?*	*Spider Silk*
Bees and Beelines	*How You Talk*	*Straight Hair, Curly Hair*
Birds at Night	*It's Nesting Time*	*A Tree Is a Plant*
Corn Is Maize	*Ladybug, Ladybug, Fly Away Home*	*Water for Dinosaurs and You*
Digging Up Dinosaurs	*Look at Your Eyes*	*Wild and Woolly Mammoths*
A Drop of Blood	*Me and My Family Tree*	*What Happens to a Hamburger*
Ducks Don't Get Wet	*My Five Senses*	*What I Like About Toads*
Fireflies in the Night	*My Visit to the Dinosaurs*	*What Makes Day and Night*
Follow Your Nose	*No Measles, No Mumps for Me*	*What the Moon Is Like*
Fossils Tell of Long Ago	*Oxygen Keeps You Alive*	*Why Frogs Are Wet*
Hear Your Heart	*The Planets in Our Solar System*	*Your Skin and Mine*
High Sounds, Low Sounds	*The Skeleton Inside You*	
How a Seed Grows	*The Sky Is Full of Stars*	

Wild and Woolly Mammoths
Copyright © 1977 by Aliki Brandenberg
Library of Congress Catalog Card Number: 76-18082
Library ISBN 0-690-01276-4
Trophy ISBN 0-06-445005-8
First Harper Trophy edition, 1983.

Wild and Woolly Mammoths

Thousands of years ago, a wild and woolly beast
  roamed the northern part of the earth.
It had two great, curved tusks
  and a long, hairy trunk.
Its big bones were covered with tough skin
  and soft fur.
The long hair on its humped back reached
  almost to the ground.
It looked like an elephant, but it was not quite as
  big.
It was a woolly mammoth.

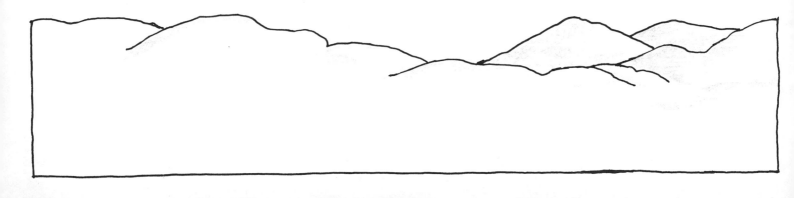

Hundreds of woolly mammoths lived during the
    last Ice Age.
Long before then, the earth was hot and swampy.
That was when the dinosaurs lived.

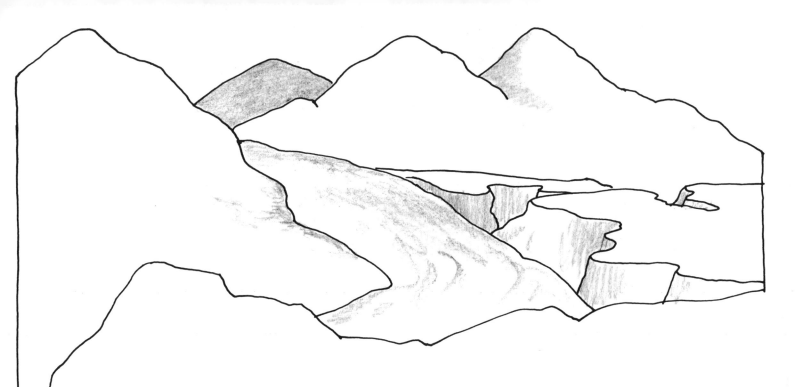

Slowly, the earth grew cold.
Some places in the north were so cold
   the snow never melted.
It formed into great rivers of ice called glaciers.

Many animals died out because of the cold.
That is probably what happened to the dinosaurs.
Other animals did not die out, but went
  south, where it was warmer.
Still others stayed in the cold north.

Some of the animals which lived during the Ice Age.

Many animals of the Ice Age grew
    heavy coats of hair.
The hair protected them from the cold.
The woolly mammoth was one of these.
It lived in what is now Europe,
    and in China, Siberia, and Alaska.

BISON

WOOLLY MAMMOTH

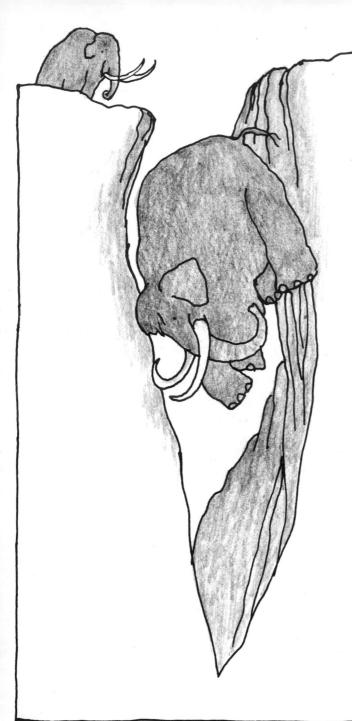

One day, a woolly mammoth
   fell into a deep crack
   in a glacier.
It broke some bones and died.
Snow and ice covered its body.
Thousands of years passed.
Slowly the weather grew warmer
   again.
The Ice Age ended.
Ice began to melt.

In 1901, the mammoth's body was discovered
   in Siberia.
Part of it was showing above the ice.
Men passing by noticed their dogs sniffing
   the rotting flesh.

Scientists uncovered the body.
Most of it was still frozen.
That part was perfectly fresh.
Dogs ate some of the meat, and liked it,
    even though it was more than 10,000 years old.

The food the mammoth had eaten before it
   died was still in its stomach.
And what food!
There were about thirty pounds of flowers,
   pine needles, moss, and pine cones.

Later, scientists tasted mammoth flesh, too,
and lived to brag about it.

Now scientists know a
   great deal about this
   ancient animal,
   even though the last one
   died thousands of
   years ago.
Scientists found more
   frozen woolly mammoths.
They found other kinds
   of mammoths, too.

The imperial mammoths lived 3 million years
    before the woolly mammoths.
At first the imperial mammoths were about
    the size of a pony.
But by the time of the woolly mammoths
    they had become the biggest mammoths of all.

Imperial mammoths were not hairy.
They didn't need to be.
They lived in the warmest parts of the world.
They lived in giant forests.
Their teeth were flat, like those of the woolly mammoth—
    perfect to grind and crush leaves and twigs.

The Colombian mammoth lived in a warmer climate, too.
It traveled from Asia to Europe, and to parts of America.

Sometimes it is called the
Jeffersonian mammoth.
It was named after Thomas
Jefferson, who was
president when one was
discovered in the
United States.
President Jefferson was
interested in the past.
He encouraged scientists to
find out more about it.

Thomas Jefferson collected bones
of ancient animals.

Mammoths were mammals.
All mammals are warm-blooded.
They usually have hair.
They have milk to nurse their young.

Mice, bats, monkeys, bears, and whales are mammals.

So are human beings.

Mammoths were the giant land mammals of
   their time.
They roamed quietly in groups.
Mammoths were peaceful plant eaters.
They did not have to hunt other animals for food.
But they had enemies.
One was the fierce saber-toothed tiger.

There were other enemies, too.
Man was the mammoth's greatest enemy.
Inside dark, damp caves scientists found out
   how important the mammoth was to early man.
They discovered paintings of mammoths on cave walls.

They found clay figures and bone carvings
  of mammoths and other animals.
They knew no animal made them.
They were made by early people who lived
  in the caves.
They were made in the days of the mammoth
  hunters, more than 25,000 years ago.
These hunters used tools made of stone,
  so we call their time the Stone Age.

These are some of the things
found in caves in France.

Woolly mammoth carved in stone

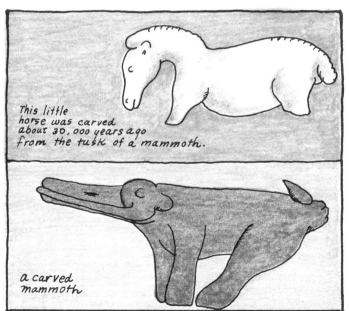

This little
horse was carved
about 30,000 years ago
from the tusk of a mammoth.

a carved
mammoth

Bone knife
carved with
bison and plants.

A whole Stone Age village was found in
Czechoslovakia and dug up.

Archaeologists, who are scientists who study
ancient ruins, learned a lot from this village and
others like it.

They learned more about mammoth hunters and
how they lived.

This is what they found out.

Mammoth hunters left the caves where they lived
in the winter.

In the spring they moved to river valleys where
herds of mammoths roamed.

They made tents in the valleys to be near the
mammoths.

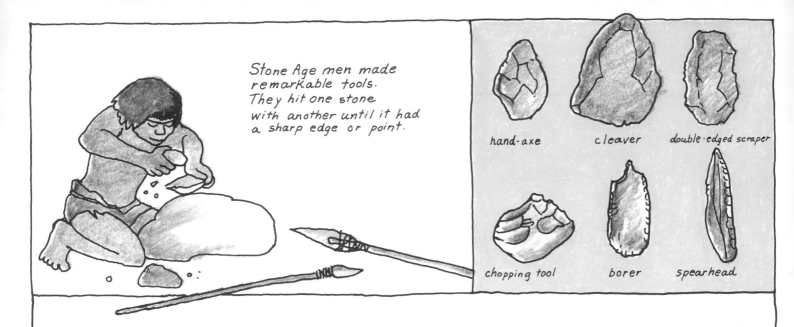

Stone Age men made remarkable tools. They hit one stone with another until it had a sharp edge or point.

hand-axe cleaver double-edged scraper

chopping tool borer spearhead

The mammoth hunters made knives and other
   tools of stone.
They used wooden spears with sharp stone points
   to kill the mammoths.
But first they had to trap them.
Sometimes the hunters made fires around the herds.
Then they forced the frightened mammoths down
   steep cliffs.
Other hunters waited at the bottom to kill the
   mammoths with their spears.

Sometimes the mammoth
hunters dug deep pits.
They covered the pits
with branches and earth.

When a mammoth
walked over the pit,
the branches broke,
and the mammoth fell in.

It could not escape.
Hunters rolled heavy stones
down on it and killed
the trapped mammoth.

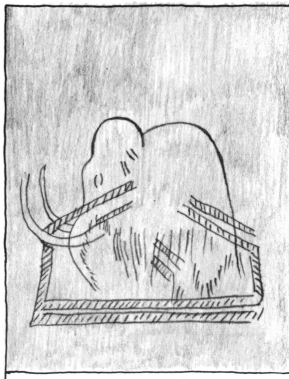

Many mammoths found showed that their bones had been broken.

This Stone Age painting was found on a wall in a cave in France.

Some people think it shows a mammoth caught in a pit trap.

The hunters and their families ate the
  mammoth meat.
They crushed the skulls and ate the brains.

They used the bones to
make tent frames.

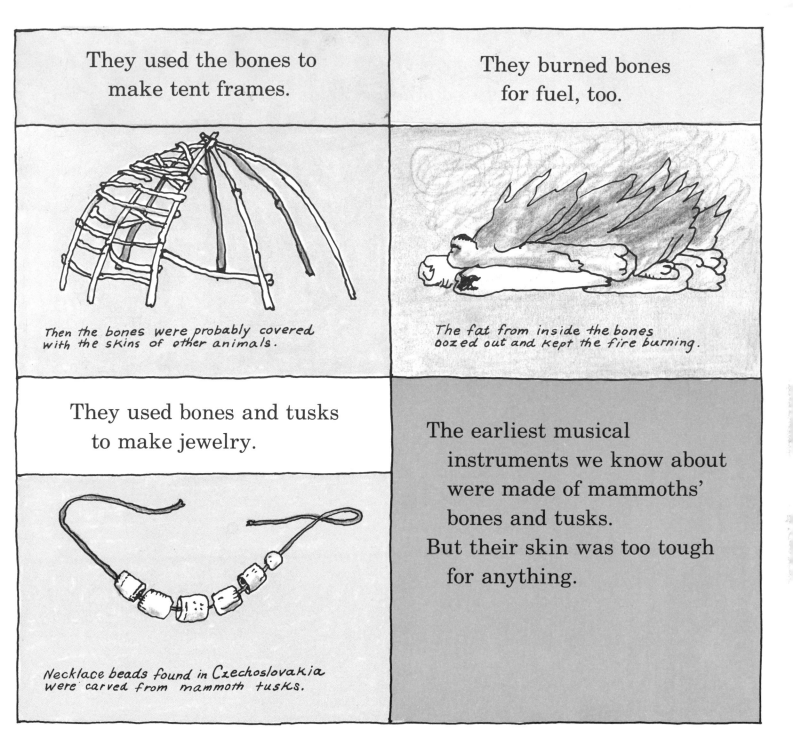

Then the bones were probably covered
with the skins of other animals.

They burned bones
for fuel, too.

The fat from inside the bones
oozed out and kept the fire burning.

They used bones and tusks
to make jewelry.

Necklace beads found in Czechoslovakia
were carved from mammoth tusks.

The earliest musical
instruments we know about
were made of mammoths'
bones and tusks.
But their skin was too tough
for anything.

These people hunted other animals, too.
The woolly rhinoceros and the giant sloth lived then.
Today they are extinct.

But bison, reindeer,

horses, and foxes,

which also lived then, have not died out.

Mammoths were hunted for a long time.
There were plenty of them, and one mammoth
  was enough to feed many families.
Today there are no mammoths.
Some people think it was the mammoth
  hunters who killed them all.
Perhaps they died out when the climate
  grew too warm.

No one knows.
But not one live woolly mammoth has
  been seen for 11,000 years.

About the Author-Illustrator

Aliki Brandenberg has been interested in ancient life for a long time. This book is a result of a letter she received from a young reader, who had learned about a mammoth feast in *Fossils Tell of Long Ago* and asked, "Whatever happened to the woolly mammoth?"

Aliki grew up in Philadelphia and was graduated from the Philadelphia College of Art. She is the author of many other popular books in the Let's-Read-and-Find-Out series, including *My Visit to the Dinosaurs* and *Corn Is Maize*, which was named First Prize Book for 1976 by the New York Academy of Sciences.

Long-time residents of New York City, Aliki and her husband, Franz, also a children's-book author, now live with their children, Jason and Alexa, in London.